198 Days

The Hardest Days Can Be Painfully Beautiful

Tracey Batchelder

198 Days: The Hardest Days Can Be Painfully Beautiful

Cover Design by Kelly Teno, Trüce Creative
www.trücecreative.com

Edited by Kristina Sky
www.skytina.com

Printed in United States of America, First Edition

ISBN   978-1-7328100-2-0

This book was written to honor

God, my Mother and my Father.

And is dedicated to

my husband, Larry, and

my children Gary, Corey and Kristin.

You were all put in my life to make me a better person.

Something only unconditional love can do.

Table of Contents

Table of Contents..5

Foreword...7

Acknowledgements...9

Chapter One
The Bonfire..13

Chapter Two
Hellooooooo??????????......................................21

Chapter Three
God Spoke...29

Chapter Four
Daddy...35

Chapter Five
Mama..45

Chapter Six
The Middle Child...63

Chapter Seven

The 6th Sense 69

Chapter Eight

Love thy Neighbor 73

Chapter Nine

Who Put "FUN" in Dysfunction? 77

Chapter Ten

Army of Advocates 83

Epilogue

Home Bittersweet Home 91

In Memory of

My 11-Pound Superhero 95

Letter from the Author 101

Foreword

Let's break this down. 198 days equals out to 6 months, 2 weeks, 1 day, 8 hours, 39 minutes and 59 seconds.

At times, this seems like a lot of time filled with memories, experiences, wins, losses, first times, and possibly second chances. And then other times, it goes by in the blink of an eye.

We all know that time is important. But understanding the value of time is what makes the difference in a lifetime.

In 198 Days, Tracey beautifully shares her life story and how a specific time frame brought her powerful life lessons on the importance of being present and awakened to what's most important in the gift we have all been given. This gift called LIFE.

I believe that as you read every word and turn every page, you will feel as if you are sitting across the table from a friend as she speaks life, hope and healing into the situation you may be facing right now.

Tracey's stirring message will show you the true meaning of turning beauty from ashes, being introduced to unconditional love, and that new beginnings are truly possible...even in endings.

This book you now hold in your hands will bring an understanding of what a transformed life looks like, stir up passion and compassion within you, and cause you to rise up into the greatest understanding of how much you are loved, valued and needed in this generation.

Get ready for your own personal encounter and journey of 198 days!

Cynda Harris, CLC

Founder & Lead Coach for Grow Life, Inc.

Life & Leadership Coach for Women

www.growandflourish.com

Acknowledgments

First and foremost, I must thank God for tapping me with a 2 X 4! He changed my life. He knew what was ahead of me and prepared me for it. I thank Him every day for making me see just how precious life is and giving me the opportunity to live my best life.

My life coach, Cynda Harris, without her mentorship and guidance I would not be the person I am today.

My editor, Kristina Sky, who went above and beyond for me. Without her, this book would not have been possible.

My wonderful, loving family. Larry, Gary, Corey and Kristin, you are all so very adored and each one of you are a treasure in my life. Thank you for your, love, kindness and support. You make me a better person every day. I love you all more than I could ever show you.

And of course, Mama and Daddy. You are forever in my heart and the lessons you have taught me will be my inspiration until I see you again.

THE JOURNEY

Chapter One

The Bonfire

12/31/2013

I am about to tell you something you may find hard to believe. It still sounds crazy to me, but crazy it is not.

The fact that it was New Year's Eve is irrelevant. Whenever I had the next day off work, you can bet I was ready to get my drink on and have fun. Larry, my husband, Corey, my middle son, and Kristin, my youngest and only daughter, who had a friend sleeping over, and I were hanging out at home. We tried to pull together a last-minute holiday party, but it didn't pan out and it was just the five of us.

That was a party as far as I was concerned, and we were going to have fun! The music went up and the beer went down. As was the norm, I was all up in everyone's business "helping" them to have fun; they loved it (NOT!).

I went into Corey's room where he was hanging with his 300,000+ Tumblr followers. I jumped up and down on his bed, took selfies with him, positioned myself in front of his computer camera, and talked to whoever he was chatting with at the time. That was me, the self-described uber-cool mom. My efforts at getting him out of his room were futile; he was just too busy.

So off to Kristin I went and shouted, "Let's take pictures!" After we took the perfect picture to post on Facebook and a few more beers in, us girls went outside where Larry was making the best fire ever. The incredible red, orange, blue and white flames must have been at least seven feet tall! We could feel the heat on our faces from twenty feet away. Our excitement grew before we even reached the firepit; we rushed back in the house and pulled out all the makings for Super S'mores because well yes, it's the perfect pairing with beer and a bonfire, for me anyway. The girls were drinking cola (I wasn't THAT cool)!

We made our s'mores, laughed, took more, not-so-perfect pictures, laughed s'more (one of many corny jokes), and were just being silly. Fun, fun, fun! Then it happened, I got this great idea! I hurried into Corey's room and insisted, "Come outside with us. Grab your laptop and bring your friends." I knew it was the only way he was going to leave that room.

I grabbed a bunch of paper and pens and told my gang, "This is what we are going to do; we are going to write down the bad stuff we want to leave behind in 2013 and the good stuff we are looking forward to and hoping to change in 2014."

After the *oh boy, here she goes* faces were exchanged, we all started writing. I have to say they were and still are very good sports about humoring me. They finished their lists and sat patiently waiting for me. Finally, Kristin was like, "Geez mom, are you writing a book?"

I must be honest; I had quite the laundry list of bad stuff. When I finally finished, I looked up at all of them and said, "Ok, crumple up your papers and throw them in the fire. All of the bad stuff will be returned to the fiery pits of Hell, and the smoke will carry our words of hope straight up to God."

Corey, who was at an age where he had little interest in "family stuff" shrugged his shoulders and looked at me like, whatever Mom, as he threw his paper into the fire. Larry, who supported me no matter what I was up to, grinned, shook his head, and tossed his paper ball in. The girls, I want to believe, were a little expectant and excited and threw their papers in together.

I, of course, had to be very dramatic and do this with finesse and flair, as if I were tossing a rose onto the stage of a beautiful ballet performance, aaaaaaannnnndddd completely missed the fire. Now I had everyone's attention, and as they were all rolling with laughter, I humbly bent over, picked up my paper and tossed it in the fire as I received their sarcastic applause. Go me!

Sounds pretty simple and fun, right? Here is where the crazy part comes in; I have not had a single drop of alcohol since that night!

Now I can't tell you exactly what I wrote that night, mostly because I was drunk, and I don't remember. Did I write that on my list? Did my family write it on theirs? I don't know! However, what I believe is, the Holy Spirit gave me instructions and God delivered me from alcohol. Oh, I can see some eyes rolling and heads shaking. I also see some of you praising God and thanking Him for what He did in my life that night.

Don't get me wrong, I know many people who have given up alcohol after it brought them to rock bottom, and they had lost so much in their lives. Many of them used AA and the 12-step program. I also went through the program via court order after a DUI. Yes, I have driven drunk a gazillion times, but I got caught once; I am so grateful that I never hurt anyone or myself. As soon as I fulfilled all the requirements that the Judge handed down and spent thousands of dollars, I celebrated, you guessed it, by drinking and probably a lot more than before the incident.

I worked with a group of people I adored and still do; we would go across the street from the office and have drinks on Fridays. It was so much fun! I loved it and wanted it to happen every week. One morning, on my way to work, I had the radio on and kept hearing about all these wonderful causes. I thought, *I need a cause.* Now bear with me… this was my actual thought process. After a little brainstorming, I came up with a worthy cause, HHA, Happy Hour Awareness. *Yes, that's it,* I thought, and from there, in my mind it grew into something worthwhile.

I went into the office and shared my cause. My co-workers loved it; they were on board. I gave bracelets to my friends that said, "Happy Hour, Bottoms Up, etc." Well, they were actually bands that went around wine glasses. This was my guarantee it would be a weekly occurrence. Yes, we had fun! Heck, isn't that what life's about? You have one life, you have to enjoy it, right?

Some nights were great, some not so great, depending on how I felt the night should go or how the alcohol hit me. Tons of memories and stories were made. Unfortunately, those kinds of friendships are not solid. We have all since moved on to other jobs and although we kind of keep in touch on social media, and I do truly care about every one of them, it's not how it used to be when we were all pulled together because of the job, and of course, the cause.

Partying was at the top of my list, without taking my family into consideration. The hours and days I missed with my family I will never get back. I know I hurt them and most likely caused my children many issues and did not lead my children by the example of how I wanted them to live their lives. I know I gave them love and great qualities, but oh I could have done so much better. They are grown now, and I don't know if it is because of me or despite me, that they are all such amazing people; I am so very proud of each one of them.

I remember being out with friends after I no longer drank. One of my very good friends slid next to me and whispered, "OK, spill it sister, why did you really stop drinking? Was it a DUI? Did Larry give you an ultimatum?"

16

I told my friend what I just told you and she looked at me like I was crazy and didn't buy it one bit. I don't know if she believes me to this day.

At first and still now, many of my friends and acquaintances feel uncomfortable with the new me. I don't blame them; I was uncomfortable with the new me. I didn't know how to act at get-togethers without a beer in my hand and alcohol to break down the walls of inhibition. Fortunately, that has passed for me; I'm not sure about them, but I don't know how to fix that.

I love my friends whether or not they drink; there is no judgment from me. Perhaps they don't find me as fun, or maybe because my priorities have changed, they can't relate to me as they did before. We all have to live out our lives as we want to or see fit.

Do I want my loved ones to find the same kind of relationship with God that I have found? You better believe I do, but that's between them and God. I know while they are living out their own stories, they will have experiences that will bring them to God. I will do what I'm supposed to do, and I will keep them in my heart and love them.

I have never had withdrawals, or any desire to drink at all, since the bonfire. Of course, this confused me. I didn't even think I wanted to quit, so to make sure, I joined a Celebrate Recovery class that the church around the corner was offering. The ladies there were all struggling and dealing with some very hard issues and I wasn't struggling at all, although I had and still have issues that are being resolved or haven't completely surfaced yet. I often thought, *I don't belong here*. I felt like an intruder, guilty for listening to their stories, yet I was encouraged and inspired by the faith and strength of each woman there.

I cannot express to you just how happy I am that my family was with me for my bonfire shenanigans or they would think I was a total wackadoodle too! However, as time went on and they saw the changes occurring in me and a transformation taking place, it allowed them to share in my belief.

They all knew that I couldn't or wouldn't have quit drinking just like that. They've lived with me while I quit smoking cigarettes and a very feeble attempt at giving up my beloved soda; they can attest it was not nearly as fun as our bonfire night.

I believe that's what God does, He shows up and does a miraculous thing, something that can't be explained, but definitely happens. It has to be something big to get our attention and to make sure He gets the credit for such a blessing. With me, He made sure to take away something I believed I enjoyed and was currently doing and then I thought, *well I gave up alcohol, I'll give up smoking.*

He very patiently waits, until you realize you do not have the strength on your own to give up any vice without help. That's how I believe He got through to me anyway; I praise Him every day for Tracey 2.0 and truly give Him all the glory.

I still don't completely understand what happened to me around that New Year's Eve bonfire but, I know, that I know, that I know from the center of my soul that God delivered me, Amen!

Jesus replied,
"You do not realize now what I am doing,
but afterward you will understand."

JOHN 13:7

Chapter Two

Hellooooooo?????????

Not only did the drinking stop, but I started to notice other changes happening from the inside out.

I had a tendency to curse like a sailor, tell dirty jokes, get the dirt on people, and have little to no respect for authority. I could go on and on, but I'll spare you the tedious list of my flaws. All of that stopped for the most part. I traded them for a new passion. I wanted to learn more about God. I started going to church, reading and talking to others who believed in the power of God. I was told this was the honeymoon phase for those who are beginning to build their faith.

People and events were placed in my path. I noticed workshops being offered on my social media feed. I wanted to attend all of them, but only signed up for those I could work around my schedule. I didn't know anyone at the first workshop I went to, but the atmosphere was warm and inviting. Everyone was so nice, and I felt very welcomed.

I was captivated as the speaker bravely shared her story. After she spoke, she went around the room and chatted with every lady in attendance. She was so likable, her compassionate personality was absolutely contagious, and I felt an immediate connection with her. This awesome woman eventually became my life coach and I still meet with her to this day.

That first year was a whirlwind of learning, meeting new people and finding myself through God. My thought process began to change along with my behaviors. It's easy to loosen up and feel confident by adding alcohol; this was so different. It took me quite a while but once I got past the habit of dependency, turns out I was there all along. I have never been more confident and find it less necessary to please everyone and need everyone to like me, which really took a lot of weight off my shoulders.

The second and third years were much different; I felt like my life was in limbo and very unsettled. God didn't seem quite as close as he had been the first year. I had a choice to make; I could very easily go back to my old life, or push through, pray and continue to grow as a Christian.

I listened to worship music, asked other believers if they had ever felt like God left them and continued to look for workshops and have sessions with my life coach. She hosted group events and I attended all that I could. She often talked about us being in a season to birth something new. I told a friend, "She's talking about birthing, but I feel like I haven't even dropped an egg!"

Yet I still pushed, not like labor pushing, but doing what I thought would please God; I wanted to experience what I saw other people living.

So it went for those two years and I kept asking God, "OK, now what? What am I supposed to do? What is the great thing I'm going to birth?"

Chirp, chirp! Chirp, chirp! Crickets! That's what I heard, nothing, no answers, not even a teeny tiny clue.

Hellooooooooo??????? God, are you still around? I'm waiting for guidance but I'm really starting to feel abandoned.

In November of 2016, my Mom was having surgery, and I made a trip to Michigan because I knew she would need some help.

She was going to have a procedure done to insert an AV Fistula on the inside of her left arm in preparation for the future dialysis she would need at some point because her kidneys weren't functioning as they should.

As I pulled up to my parents' home, Dad was waiting in the garage, as always, to greet me and help with my bags. It took only a glance to notice how thin he had become, and I was startled as the word, cancer, echoed in my head. As I hugged him, I couldn't bring myself to say anything to him other than, "Where's the rest of you?"

"Looks like I gave it to you," he laughed.

Yes, thank you, Dad, I sarcastically thought to myself. I thought we weren't supposed to blatantly throw it out there when a woman put on a few extra pounds. After all, I was at an age where "the change" had started, and the biggest change I'd experienced so far was weight gain, and well, maybe a mood swing here and there. Rather than speaking my thoughts, I just laughed with him.

Mom's surgery was the next day, so we just visited and caught up on what was happening. "How are the kids doing?" "We get eight to ten deer out in the back field every day!" "This or that bird has been coming around, but those darned ole blue jays are mean as heck and scare them off," etc.

Just the usual small talk followed by an early bedtime because we had to have Mom at the surgery center by 6 o'clock in the morning.

Dad and I waited together while mom went through outpatient surgery and we brought her home when she was finally discharged. She couldn't use her arm and we had a difficult time getting her in the house. After a few unsuccessful attempts, Dad finally put ramps up against the patio at the back of the house, and we managed to get her and her walker up the ramps and into the house.

Once Mom was settled, Dad and I had a few moments to ourselves; he broke down and cried. He had become her caregiver. He helped her with her socks and shoes every day, fixed her meals, did all the shopping and more. My heart broke as with tears streaming down his cheeks, he hopelessly shook his head and told me, "I don't know how much longer I can take care of her."

I hugged him and told him he was doing a great job with her. He sighed and put his head in his hands. He looked so defeated; we were both so tired from the long day. Mom was sleeping so I suggested we get some sleep and things would look better in the morning. He agreed, but my suggestion also caught me off guard. My mom had said that to me so many times over the years when I would call her when something was upsetting me, or I found myself facing a dilemma. She would say, "Go get a good night's sleep and things will look better in the morning."

I believe her mother had given her the very same advice. I thought, oh my goodness it's happening, I'm becoming my mother!

I had called my parents often to check in before my trip, but what you see in person is a whole lot different than what you hear on a phone call. I could see Dad was in pain, and he had COPD so he would easily get out of breath while he helped mom. I also noticed he had started using a cane at all times. When my mother would help him, she had a walker which added to the challenges for her. I was amazed by how they truly depended on each other, what one couldn't do the other did. They were a team.

I was a bit amused by the bickering and faces they made behind each other's back; I just pretended not to notice. There were times I had to leave the room so I wouldn't laugh because sometimes it was like watching a sitcom, except to them it was a serious matter.

You know, like when my 4'9" mom asked my dad three times to get a bowl down for her, but he didn't hear her because he wasn't wearing his hearing aids, and when he finally realized she was talking to him, he would roll his eyes and say something like, "You just had to ask, I'm not a mind reader ya know," knowing good and well she had asked and he didn't hear her.

I stayed to help for a week, but it didn't feel like enough. I returned home filled with worry about how my parents were making do and began to brainstorm ways I could make life a little easier on them. I decided to order the things they used through Amazon Pantry, but it backfired. I called every night to check on them. Unfortunately, one night I chose to call at the very moment the first box was dropped on their doorstep. I always have had a great sense of timing.

Mom answered the phone and I could hear Dad grumbling and struggling to get the box in the house. It was too heavy!! Out of breath, I heard him say "Tell her not to do that again. I can manage my own shopping, thank you very much!" Ouch, that didn't go quite as planned.

During the month of December, I continued to call every day, and I heard things I didn't like at all!

On one call she told me my dad was very upset because his jeep wouldn't start, and he was waiting for a friend to come help him because he couldn't lift the hood. That was so hard for me to hear as I always thought of Dad as the strongest man ever. He could do anything, fix anything or make anything, yet now he didn't have the strength to lift the hood on his jeep to replace a dead battery.

Mom very casually told me she had fallen in the kitchen and dad couldn't pick her up, so he covered her with a blanket and called the fire department. The wonderful firemen came out to the house, picked her up, checked her all out and then helped her to bed. This would not be the last time the fire department was called; she fell twice more, once in the bathroom and again in the kitchen. At this point, she was on a first-name basis with her rescuers, Dan and Dan. She didn't just call them that, it was, in fact, their names. It was not unusual at all for the same responders to come to the house every time.

The little town they lived in literally had one blinking light at the main, and only, intersection. There was a gas station on one corner, across the street was the town hall and on the opposite corner was a grocery/liquor/pizza place. I was floored when mom called and ordered a pizza and asked them, "When you bring the pizza, will you also bring me a bottle of cough syrup and a bottle of Jim Beam for Loren?"

You know what? They did!! Once I knew the fabulous people were willing to do this, I have to admit, I requested non-pizza items a couple of times. It was like real-time Amazon! There was a post office and of course the fire station. I loved this little town, let me clarify, I appreciated this little town as an adult, I hated it as a kid. When I left home the population was 423 minus me.

These calls upset me so much and I felt so helpless. I was exactly 1,176 miles away from them!

My aunt, Mom's sister, cleaned my parents' house once a month for them. I knew she would help anytime she could, yet every time I suggested to my mom to call my aunt or my sister, she would make an excuse not to or just insist she didn't want to bother them. Even though I knew help was just a phone call away, I also knew they wouldn't pick up the phone and ask for help unless there was a crisis and at that point, it would be Dan and Dan they would call to the rescue.

I couldn't focus on anything! I had a constant nagging fear that something was going to happen, and I wasn't going to be there for them. It was internal torture; I had to find a way to be certain my parents were safe and well-cared for.

In an attempt to do something, I sent a group chat to a few family members and explained the difficulties mom and dad were having and asked if they would take turns visiting them once a week to check on them and see if they needed help with anything. You would have thought I asked them to commit a crime! Matter of fact, I probably would have gotten a lot less backlash had I asked them to commit a crime.

I was told I was trying to take away their independence and I would have them in a home and they would end up dying there. WHAT???!! I couldn't believe what I was hearing, it went back and forth until one of them finally said they would make a trip once a week. That never happened.

I was getting a glimpse of what I was being prepared to do, but I didn't realize it at the time.

God does say, "Ask and it shall be given to you;
seek and you will find; knock and the door will be opened."

MATTHEW 7:7-8

Chapter Three

God Spoke

2/8/2017

God's timing is everything; I knew he heard me when I was feeling lost and not knowing my next step, even though all I heard was nothing. You can't rush God or slow him down; when He appoints a time for something, it's just plain non-negotiable.

My mom called me while I was at work, something she never would do unless it was an emergency. My heart was already racing when I said, "Hello." I knew it would be bad news, I just didn't know to what extent the badness would be. I braced myself and listened as mom told me my dad had been admitted to the hospital. I immediately heard in my head, "GO!"

This was the first time I knew I was hearing God speak to me; I had no doubt! The only thing I can say is, it wasn't my inside head voice, ya know the one that you hear when you're thinking.

I immediately headed over to my supervisor's desk. She could tell right away I was upset. I told her, "My dad has been admitted to the hospital. I need to get to him right away. I need to go home and make arrangements to leave no later than tomorrow."

She was very sympathetic and understanding. "Let us know if you need anything," she assured me.

"I'll let you know what's happening as soon as I know," I responded as I gathered my belongings and quickly left the office.

God's voice was so clear, I bought a one-way ticket for the first time in my life. I knew I had to, "GO", but I had no clue when I might return. I arrived in Detroit at 9:30 the very next morning, hurried off the plane and gathered my luggage with a sense of urgency. The driver I had hired was at the curb ready for me, but I couldn't get to the house fast enough.

Finally, we were pulling into the driveway. The absence of my dad waiting in the garage for me made my heart ache. I walked through the garage door, and the moment mom saw me a look of relief flickered through her eyes, but not quite enough to cover the worry. Mom didn't typically show a lot of emotion, so the fact she looked fearful made my tears start to flow as I hugged her tight.

My sister had arrived earlier, dropped off by her husband. She was unable to drive due to health issues, and both her and my mom had been waiting for me to drive them to the hospital. Remembering how difficult it was to get my mom in the car, I quickly loaded everything she had packed for dad before I helped her to the car. Then we were on our way to see dad.

They lived in the country, so we had a 45-minute drive, with very little talking other than my mom being my GPS for directions to the hospital. I made her chuckle when I told her she should be the voice on the map app. As a matter of fact, she gave me more notice than any app ever has when I had to turn right at the next light.

I honestly couldn't wait to get to the hospital and see dad with my own eyes. We walked in the hospital room and he was wide awake. True to his disposition, he looked at me and said, "Oh hon, you didn't need to come all the way up here."

As he spoke, I couldn't get over how frail he was. The moment stood still as I looked at my larger-than-life dad, so frail and so small. Through my tears I could barely respond, "Yes, yes, I did."

I knew I was right where I was supposed to be.

Doctors, nurses, and other medical staff busied in and out of the room, examining dad, giving medications, and ordering tests. Dad wasn't aggravated or irritable at all, which confirmed to me just how badly he was feeling. Whenever he was in the hospital, if he started feeling better, he became grouchy and insisted it was time to go home. Until he would get discharged, he was not happy with one person and well, they would become less fond of him.

I want to take a moment and give kudos to nurses; all they do and all they put up with is incredible! For the most part, the hospital staff I interacted with were amazing. We waited all day and into the evening for test results or any kind of information we could get. Unfortunately, we were informed, "We won't know anything until tomorrow."

We stayed on and visited with dad until it was very obvious he was ready for us to go home. Mom hated when dad was in the hospital and worried about him being all alone; she wanted to be there all day, every day, morning to night. Dad, on the other hand, would've preferred we came daily, talked to the doctors, gathered information and went on our way. I think he felt if we were there, he had to entertain us, and it prevented him from the sleep and rest he so needed.

After convincing mom to leave, we faced the next challenge-getting her out to the car, in and out of the car, and up the two flights of steps and into the house with her walker. This was a challenge we would repeat over and over throughout my stay every time we went anywhere. She hated the ordeal, it caused her tremendous pain and physically drained her.

Despite the difficulties, we ended up with a great system when it was just her and I. Honestly, it was more like a circus act, and sometimes we laughed so hard we could barely breathe, but it worked for us.

When we arrived home, I fixed up an evening snack and meds for mom. Then it was time to bag up the additional items dad wanted, along with mom's snacks and meds for the next day. She was a diabetic and we had to be very careful she ate often and had her insulin with her always. There were times her blood sugar was very high or very low, and we had to call paramedics. If they could stabilize her to an acceptable number, they would let her stay home, if not, to the hospital she would go. I couldn't even begin to imagine what it would be like if both dad and mom ended up in the hospital at the same time.

As I said, I had no doubt God spoke to me. So much happened, and I remained calm and confident through most of it. I am not the person you want in a crisis, unless getting very upset and crying are called for in the situation, I am not your girl, but I had strengths I do not typically possess. I can tell you now that He was with me through every step.

As we go along on this journey, I think you will notice some things that will make you go hmmmm. A plane ride, a car ride, a trip to the hospital and back to the house, may not seem like all that much to talk about, but I can testify it is a jam-packed and exhausting day.

This was just the beginning of day one and the first day of a journey I will cling to for the rest of my life.

"So shall my word be that goes out of my mouth; it shall not return to me empty, but it shall accomplish that which I purpose, and shall succeed in the thing for which I sent it."

ISAIAH 55:11

Chapter Four

Daddy

My Daddy could do anything, fix anything and make anything. For my entire life, he has been my hero. I know my dad had flaws as we all do, yet when I remember him, it's his goodness, kindness and his love for me that is there. Nothing else matters in my heart.

Nothing can prepare you to be your parents' caregiver. Oh yeah, I've raised three humans and they turned out pretty darn good. But because you are a parent does not mean you are naturally equipped to care for your parents. I can honestly say it was the hardest thing I've ever done in my life.

Dad was never without his hearing-aids; they were usually in his pocket or on the table next to him. That's why when the doctor came in to tell us they had found cancer on dad's esophagus, he couldn't hear a word. While the doctor spoke, dad nodded in understanding. When the doctor asked if he had any questions, he said, "No."

The doctor left the room and mom turned to him, "Did you hear everything?"

He shrugged, "Some of it," which meant none of it.

Mom turned to me, "Tracey?" I knew by the look in her eyes, she couldn't bring herself to repeat it.

He looked so discouraged as I told him they found cancer. The worst part of this, is then I had to repeat, "Unfortunately, you are not a candidate for treatment," and watched all hope drain from his face.

At the time he weighed a mere 128 pounds, and he was just too frail to make it through surgery or to tolerate chemo or radiation.

As this devastating news sunk in, the nurse walked cheerily into the room, "Well, hi there, mister, what do you have to say for yourself?"

Dad looked up at her matter-of-factly, "I have cancer."

She gently took his hand, "I know, and I am so sorry."

Dad was in the hospital about a week and was discharged with an order for a PET scan. Our orders were to keep him as comfortable as possible. We took him to have the test done, the nurse took him back and within 30 minutes a nurse brought him back out. Poor guy! He had a panic attack. He looked right at me and said, "Get me the hell out of here and take me home."

At first, he was quiet on the way home. The silence was interrupted when he tearfully insisted, "I have never felt that way in my life and I am never going to again."

There would be no PET scan.

So, dad was home and we settled into a bit of a routine for his daily care. Home health nurses visited a few times a week to check his vitals and teach him a few simple exercises. He was a trooper and did everything the nurses asked him to do; he even did his exercises when the nurses weren't there. He stood in the kitchen, at the sink, and held onto the counter while he slowly lifted each leg. He was not willing to give up without a fight.

I am a pretty intuitive person, and intuition was telling me dad hadn't been feeling well for some time. I believe he had known it wasn't going to get any better. Although he didn't say anything to anyone, his actions spoke volumes.

In November when I had been up to help my mom, he was on a mission to get her a new car. He went to the dealership, asked questions, looked around and brought booklets and all the information he had found out home for mom. Shortly after I left, he bought her a brand-new Chevy Impala equipped with everything she wanted. She never drove it and he only drove it for three months and not very often.

Now that I was there, he was seriously getting his ducks in a row. He had a photo album with every car he'd ever owned, and he had yet to take a picture of the Impala. That was my first "favor." That's what he would say, "Hey Trace, if you're not too busy today, would you do me a favor?"

I photographed the Impala and we added the pictures to his treasured album. We looked at all the other vehicles in the album, while he reminisced a little about each one. He turned a page and there was our family Suburban. Daddy started to laugh, and my cheeks started to burn; uh, oh, I knew this story. "Tracey, do you remember when the Suburban caught fire and you just stood in the back screaming instead of getting out?"

Embarrassed, I thought, *Give me a break, Dad, I was five years old*, but then my memory kicked in and I was flooded with pride. "What I remember most is that my Daddy rescued me."

Dad just smiled and turned to the next page.

Then there was a bulb out on the back of his truck that needed to be replaced and I did another "favor." He was going down his mental to-do list and checking things off.

He also wanted to teach me things that needed maintaining, so as I was doing him favors, I was also learning how to maintain the generator, the sump-pump, the wood (turned gas) stove and the water softener. I loved doing these things for him, knowing he was putting his confidence in me just made me feel so good. I wasn't always the best daughter ever. But I was there now, and I wanted to do whatever I could for them. It meant everything to me to put his mind at ease.

Now I was a great day nurse, however, I sucked as a night nurse. I loved my sleep and could sleep through anything. We devised a plan to keep our cell phones within arm's-length and if either one of them needed me, they called my phone. My mom called me pretty much nightly; she needed assistance in the restroom.

A week and a half after dad came home, my phone rang at 5 o'clock in the morning. Surprisingly, it was dad. I didn't even answer the phone I just went to him and he said, "Trace, I just can't seem to get up."

When I was helping him, I realized he was burning up with fever. I helped him to the bathroom and settled him back in. I woke my mom and let her know we needed to call 911 because dad had gotten worse. She got up and we called.

My dad was adamant. "I do not want to go!"

Thankfully, the paramedics convinced him it was necessary. Mom and I met the ambulance at the hospital emergency room. Dad was very agitated and kept trying to sit up, he couldn't do it by himself, but he was still determined to get out of that bed. The nurses gave him meds to calm down and when they wore off, he'd be at it again.

When we went back to the hospital the 2nd day, dad was very alert, sitting up and acting like he felt fine. We were hopeful, but also had the nurses' words lurking in the back of our minds, "Many times people will "rally" prior to passing. We've seen patients become very strong. They may even experience heightened senses."

We all talked and laughed for a while and then dad requested, "Please, take me home."

We spoke to the doctor and we all agreed. Since there was really nothing to help or heal him at the hospital, we wanted to give him his wish. He would be kept comfortable and surrounded by the home he built and the life he created with hard work and my mom by his side.

A Hospice team was called, and they met my Aunt to set the house up. We could now take care of him and he would be safe and as comfortable as possible. We headed home. We helped him into the house and the first words out of his mouth were, "I want my couch." Dad saw the hospital bed Hospice had delivered, and he wanted nothing to do with it at first.

Again, he was agitated and attempted to get up over and over, but he couldn't sit or stand by himself. We were finally able to get him to relax and he gave up his effort at trying to get up. He gave me a dirty look, stuck his tongue out at me and went to sleep.

While he slept, the Care Team tended to my mom and checked her out to make sure she was holding up okay. I was shown how to measure and administer the medication to keep dad comfortable. I had to give it to him every two hours, so I set alarms on my phone and kept a sheet of times and amounts given so the nurses would have it for their records.

The first night I was so afraid I would miss the alarm to give him the medicine, I made a little "bed" on the floor next to him and tried sleeping between the alarms. It was a long night, but we didn't miss one dose. Morning came and mom woke up and went right to him and talked for a while. I left the two of them so they could have their time to chat.

I made mom breakfast and got the medicine ready for the day.

The nurses came and did what they needed to do and since they had been there the day before and dad was started on the morphine, he slept. I asked the nurse, "Is my dad going to wake up again?"

She shook her head and told me, "It's not likely."

I don't know what hurt worse - my heart, my stomach or the lump in my throat. It was something I already had a feeling about; his breathing had changed significantly, but mom's reaction doubled the pain. It was as if she truly believed he was going to get better.

Day two at home we continued the meds, mom sat with him every minute she could and held his hand and talked with him. When she wasn't with him, I was. Even though we were giving him morphine, I believe he heard us. He would make a small noise, or his facial expression would change very briefly. It was a comfort to believe he knew we were with him every step of the way.

Dad always had the television on when he was home. He loved the western channel and it was always very loud so he could hear it when his "ears" were charging (almost all the time). He often joked, "I've turned into Mr. Potato head. I have to put on my eyes, ears and mouth every day."

We kept the TV the way we knew he liked it, as he would have had it. When night came, I put down my makeshift bed next to him and set my alarms like the night before. I was afraid he was going to slip away in between alarms. He hung on as the night seemed not to want to end. I was abruptly awakened by the TV with a rendition of "Worthy is the Lamb" that I had never heard and the TV seemed louder than before. My first thoughts were *why is church on the western channel* and *it's not even Sunday* and OH NO! *Did I miss my alarm?*

40

I looked at my phone and, no, the alarm wasn't set to go off for half an hour, it was 6:50 a.m. I got up to check on my dad. He was taking his last breaths, I held his hand, kissed him and told him I loved him, and he was gone. Yes, I truly believe God woke me up, so my dad didn't have to leave this earth alone.

These days I was living were pushing me to the end of my strength. There were so many things that I had to do, and I had never had any experiences to prepare me. Mom was still asleep, and now I had to wake her up and break the news. She got up, grabbed her walker and my heart shattered again, this time for her, as I heard her call down the hallway, "I'm coming baby."

We sat with him saying our goodbyes and just talking and remembering times we'd had over the years and when mom was ready, I called Hospice to let them know he had passed.

The nurse arrived and then the sheriff. I found out that it was mandatory when someone died at home for a deputy to file a report. They needed to confirm it was a natural death and not an assisted suicide. I'm not naming names, but it was because of a well-known doctor in Michigan.

For the two months I had been there, my dad's shoulder caused him an incredible amount of pain (he said on a scale of 1-10 it was about a 25). I continuously put on pain relief lotion or heated the rice pack and put it on his shoulder. He could not move it without crying out.

Mom and I had left the room so the nurse could unhook everything, wash him up and get him dressed. I happened to walk past the doorway right when the nurse raised his arm over his head to put his shirt on. It was the first time he didn't cry out in pain. The realization that he had been freed from pain sent me into immediate meltdown mode.

It's weird what hit me the hardest as this life event happened around me. This was a person, in my mind that was going to live forever, my invincible Daddy. As much as my heart hurt because he was gone, I also had a very real peace about it. I had helped him get from here to there.

Once my sister arrived at my parents' home, the funeral home came to pick up dad and that's when the whirlwind began - funeral arrangements, cards and photos, music and flowers and shopping for clothes.

By the time we got home from all of this, I would have my second meltdown of the day. I was exhausted after two nights of virtually no sleep, and after all the planning and picking out of everything I felt this had been by far the worst day of my life up to that point. It was only fitting that I had the worst meltdown of my life; sobbing so hard it actually hurt, forget about ugly crying, this was an absolute ratchet wailing, snot flowing, body shuddering episode.

After, there was not a thing left in me. I couldn't even eat dinner with my mom and sister. I apologized and went to bed. I knew my mom needed help and her and my sister were hurting also; I just had nothing left to give.

"Let not your heart be troubled; you believe in God, also believe in me. In my Father's house are many mansions; if it were not so, I would have told you. I go to prepare a place for you. I will come again and will receive you to Myself; that where I am, there you will be also. And where I go you know, and the way you know."

JOHN 14:1-4

Chapter Five

Mama

Losing Dad was hard on all of us, but my mom was absolutely lost without him, which is not surprising. Imagine someone at your side for 58 years and then they are just gone. Words can't fully explain that feeling, I'm sure.

The funeral preparations and then funeral itself were very difficult for her. Many people came to pay their respects. I didn't know or remember most of them, but Mom made her best effort to speak to as many as she could.

I was determined to honor my dad and speak at his funeral. Usually, I am sick afraid to speak in public. It took a lot out of me, but I was able to share words that reflected my heart with a sense of calm and peace.

Our Pastor had stopped performing services to take a full-time position in the Hospice care field. We were so grateful he made an exception for our family. There was no one else I felt was right to speak on behalf of our family but him. He conducted a beautiful service for my dad.

My sister, my mom, and I each selected a song to be played. Mom chose "Waiting on a Woman." This was beautiful and humorous. It was "their" song. Dad would tease mom, "I'm always waiting on you, at the house, at the store, and everywhere," and then he would sing, "Waiting on a woman, lalalala."

When their song ended, Mom leaned over and whispered to me, "I hope he waits for me."

With tears in my eyes, I squeezed her hand in assurance. She squeezed back and said, "I hope I don't make him wait too long."

It was a very long, very hard day for all of us.

We tried to have some sort of a routine and get used to our new normal without dad in the days and weeks following the funeral. There were doctor appointments, trips to pick up prescriptions, the normal everyday tasks and errands. We gathered all of dad's meds and turned them in to the Sheriff's department. I had asked the hospice nurse to destroy all the narcotics right away. I didn't want to take a chance they would get in the wrong hands.

We managed to make it through the first couple of weeks. Mom had a podiatrist appointment. We had breakfast and got ready for the day. Once we arrived at the doctor's office, mom was struggling to catch her breath. Inside, she sat for a while and managed to regain her normal breathing pattern.

The doctor was kind and took the time to chat with her for a bit before giving her the shots in her feet. When the procedure was finished, we were on our way. I think the bank was our next stop. Outside, mom kind of froze and would not step off the curb. She was in a panic, struggling to catch her breath again, and insisted, "I can't step down off the curb."

Somehow, I managed to help her back into the doctor's office. She sat down and gasped, "I can't breathe."

I turned to the nurse and asked, "Can you please call 911 for us?"

The paramedics arrived quickly and took over, asking questions, taking her vitals, and then we were off to the hospital.

Noooooo, I cried all the way there, I am not ready for this.

My feelings were still too raw to do this again – hospital visits, sickness, not knowing what to expect. I prayed for healing and strength and then I was there. I looked at the all too familiar entrance, took a deep breath and walked into the emergency room.

Tests revealed Mom's sugar levels were very high. She also had congestive heart failure which caused fluids to build up around her lungs, squeezing them and making breathing difficult. Her blood sugar was quickly stabilized, and she was admitted to deal with the fluids around her heart and lungs.

Shortly before this happened, my employer sent my office computer which allowed me to work remotely from Michigan. I had internet installed, the computer set up, and was ready to get back to work. This was a responsibility I did not have when I was taking care of dad.

When it feels like you already have all the stress you can handle, and more responsibility is added to your already full days, what do you do? You juggle, you shuffle, you adjust, you attempt to find your balance and hope you can get it all done without having a nervous breakdown.

That's exactly what I began to do while mom was in the hospital. I called a few times a day to check on her condition and ask if I was needed there right away. If not, I worked half a day, took an extended lunch, and hurried to the hospital for doctor updates. I was concerned about mom spending long days by herself, so I stayed and visited with her for a while. After that, I went back to the house and finished my workday. After I made a few calls to check on my family at home and to say goodnight to mom I collapsed into bed so I could get up the next day and do it all over again.

When Mom was released from the hospital, she needed

continued care and was transferred to a nursing home. My long days were on repeat for months.

Mom expressed her worry to me, "You've done nothing for yourself since you've been here. You should find a nice church to go to."

We had talked about my life changes and she wanted me to continue to grow. I knew she was right. I hadn't been to church in a while. My cousin had invited me to attend her church while I was there, and I took her up on it. It was very similar to my home church in Florida, and I loved it. It didn't change my busy schedule, but it was just what I needed to ground myself.

One Sunday, the regular pastor was attending a men's retreat. The chaplain of the Detroit Tigers baseball team just happened to be there in his place. After the service, I kind of hung around like a creeper and waited for him. When he came out of the auditorium, I introduced myself and he listened intently as I shared the events that had taken place over the last few months. I bravely asked, "Could you send an encouraging note to my mom? She's an avid Tigers fan and never misses a game on TV. I think it might brighten her day."

To my delight, he agreed, "I would be happy to do that. Here's my email address. Send me her information."

I did all that I could to keep mom's spirits up. I bought matching Tigers hats complete with girly bling, and socks and a Tigers body pillow just for her. If there was a ball game on, we made it a party. The gear came out, selfies were taken and most often we would watch the Tigers lose. Mom knew every player's name and she got fired up, shaking her head in disgust as she gave her advice to whoever just "screwed up."

When there wasn't some kind of party going on, we paid bills, watched a movie or just enjoyed some girl talk. We never ran out of things to talk about.

The residents in the nursing home could be very colorful. One of my mom's roommates was very confused and kept thinking the nurse call button was the remote for the TV. Every time she changed the station or turned up the volume, the nurses came flying in to take it from her. She looked at them indignantly and said, "It don't work anyway. You can have it." She was absolutely precious!

There were so many sweet elderly people that I just adored. Another lady dressed to the nines and wore big, bright costume jewelry every day. She greeted folks coming in and chatted with people in the halls. I decided then and there I wanted to be her when I get to that age.

There were also people who were brought to the nursing home and never had a visitor or received flowers and that broke my heart. I hope if your elders are still with you, you will treasure them until the end. I know I made mistakes, but I am so glad I was there to make them. Of course, I have beaten myself up plenty and I can't change any of those mistakes now, but oh how I wish I could.

We met with mom's care team and she cried when they informed us, she would need to be there for 3 or 4 months. Everyone was concerned and asked, "Why are you are crying?"

"I'm just thinking about your dad," she claimed, but I didn't buy it.

I suspected her tears were about our plans to travel to Florida for Kristin's graduation and party. I shared this with the care team, but they regretfully informed us that it would be dangerous for mom to travel at this stage in her recovery. They encouraged me to go with the assurance that mom would be well-cared for in my absence. My mom would never ask me to miss my daughter's graduation, but she certainly didn't want me to leave. As you can imagine, this did nothing to help the feelings that were swirling around.

There was so much to consider. I had to plan to travel with my work equipment on weekends so I could continue to work during the week. This meant I needed to leave one weekend to be home in time for the graduation, stay for another weekend for the party, and head back to Michigan on the following weekend. The idea of me being gone for three weeks went over like a lead balloon!

Mom was not one bit happy about it, but that's how it went. She had become very dependent on me. More often than not, when someone asked her a question, she looked at me to answer. My aunt and sister visited, but mom's anger turned into depression while I was away. When I returned, I hugged her and promised we would be glued at the hip from now on. She rolled her eyes and said, "Oh Boy!" That made me giggle.

While I was in Florida, I received a call from the Tigers chaplain. He asked me for the address of the nursing home. He was on his way to visit mom. WHAT?!? I was so excited. I quickly gave him the address and asked, "Could I have just one more thing?"

"What's that?" he asked.

"Have someone take a picture of you and mom together and send it to me."

He laughed, "No problem."

He arrived and found mom doing her exercises with the physical therapist. She was in her glory when he introduced himself and gave her a swag bag with a cap, calendar, and signed baseball. It was all the nurses and residents could talk about for days, and everyone treated mom like a celebrity.

I received my picture of the two of them. Mom was holding her signed baseball and her smile reached all the way to her eyes! It had been too long since I had seen her smile like that.

We spoke on the phone later that day and I asked, "Were you surprised? Did your visitor make your day?"

"Yes, I guess it was ok," was her reply.

Don't forget she was mad at me for being away. Everyone already told me how happy the visit made her, but I didn't need to hear it, a picture says so much more than words can ever say.

When I returned to Michigan, she showed me the goodies. On the baseball under the player's signature a bible verse was referenced, Mark 10:27. When I arrived back at mom's house, I looked it up. "Looking at them," Jesus said, 'With men it is impossible, but not with God, because all things are possible with God.'"

I suddenly felt very hopeful again and prayed to God to do what men couldn't and fix my mom.

When I visited mom, the nurses told me, "She is doing great. Getting stronger every day, she's even losing weight."

I was watching mom closely. I could tell when she was feeling better, and I could tell when she looked tired or uncomfortable, but I had no idea what was going on inside her body. I relied totally on the doctors and nurses for that information.

I knew I had to prepare healthier meals for her and keep her up and moving for exercise when she was well enough to leave the rehabilitation center. After three and a half months, we finally heard the words we had been waiting for. Mom was good to go home. I was so happy. She was better and we could finally start to move on.

We both had a few ideas. I thought maybe we could live like snowbirds, winters in Florida and summers in Michigan. While I was hoping for this option, I found out mom was trying to find a way to move my entire family to Michigan. She had it all figured out, "There's enough room here for everyone," she told me matter-of-factly. Moving on turned out to be quite the challenge.

She wasn't home for long when I realized she didn't improve as much it seemed when she was in the facility. Some days, she seemed worse. The first thing I noticed was she was very quiet, too quiet. I assumed it was difficult for her to be at home without dad there. I wondered if her real grieving was finally taking place. I was also concerned that her appetite had decreased. What worried me the most was that she moaned, and moaned, and moaned.

"Mom, what's wrong?" I would ask.

"I don't know," was her response.

I followed with, "What can I do to make it better?"

And again, all she said was, "I don't know."

It was a mystery to me. Her home health care team visited regularly. She did whatever they asked her to do without complaint. I told them about the moaning, in hopes they could figure it out. When asked, she shrugged her shoulders like she didn't know and said, "My back hurts, and I can't get comfortable."

We tried the bed, we tried the couch, and she always ended up back in her recliner which seemed to be where she was as comfortable as she could be.

I still had to work and take care of mom. Every morning I quickly did what needed to be done to settle mom in for the day so I could get to work – breakfast, meds, sugar check, insulin, the list goes on. One morning, she expressed, "I feel like a little kid. I need help with everything, even when I go to the bathroom."

"Mama, this is temporary," I encouraged her, "Soon enough, you'll be able to do these things on your own. It will just take time."

I didn't want her to feel as if she was a burden, but I'm pretty sure I failed at that. I know that may sound like I'm judging myself harshly, but in hindsight, I was not present most of the day and had my mom on a to-do list. While I completed one task, my mind was already on to the next two or three tasks I needed to do and planning how to get my work hours in. I would do anything to go back and change that.

Instead of check, check, check, I wish I would have had more conversations with her, taken the time to ask what was on her mind rather than just doing what needed to be done. I feel like I failed my mom. Wow, that was hard to admit!

It seemed the more time I was away from her, the worse the moaning was. When I finally fell into bed exhausted, the moaning became louder. There was very little sleep. My Aunt visited after an especially long night. She took one look at me and said, "You look awful."

I filled her in on what was going on. While she visited, I got "things" done. That night was another doosey. Mom was moaning and I tried everything – pillows, rice packs, pain-relieving lotion, nothing stopped the moaning. She insisted she didn't know why she was moaning or what I could do to help.

I thought maybe her sugar was low or high. I brought her finger stick and monitor to her, and she looked at it like she had no clue what to do with it. I helped her as well as I could and when

I gave her the insulin, she stuck that in her finger like she did to check her sugar. I asked, "Mom, are you confused?"

Her voice shook as she answered hesitantly, "Yes, I think so."

I was scared. "Mom, I think you need to go back to the hospital."

Like a small child she begged, "No, please don't make me go back there."

I didn't know what to do. I called my Aunt, and as soon as the words were out of my mouth, "I need you," she replied, "I'm on my way."

I was so tired after sleepless nights and non-stop days; I was relieved just knowing she was on her way.

When she arrived, I quietly told her what was happening, and she told mom, "I know you don't want to go, but we have to take you back to the hospital."

My mom looked right at me and said, "I just want to die."

I didn't know then, but those would be the last words she spoke to me.

The paramedics arrived quickly and before I knew it, I was following an ambulance to the emergency room, again. My aunt and I arrived, and the hospital staff already had her in a bed and were working on her.

Mom wouldn't even look at us let alone talk to us. She had said, "No, she did not want to go," and now she was mad at us. Her blood sugar had crashed to 35, and I knew this was horrible. The nurse brought in graham crackers and orange juice for her. She was too weak to feed herself. I sat by her bed, feeding her small pieces of cookie one by one, and holding the straw in the styrofoam cup of orange juice up to her lips for her to sip.

I will never forget the look in her eyes, a combination of fear, surrender, love, apology. I was overcome by the depth of emotions she conveyed to me as she nibbled on a cookie and drank her orange juice. I had to step out. My aunt stayed and continued to help her with the rest of the juice.

After I took a few moments to compose myself, I stepped out of the visitor's room and into the stark hospital hallway. I could hear her moaning in pain before I stepped back into the room. "My feet are on too tight," she begged, "Someone, please loosen my feet."

I couldn't bear her being in so much pain. I pressed the call button and asked the nurse, "Can you please give her something for the pain?"

My aunt and I sat there helplessly, holding her hands, trying to console her as her cries grew louder and louder. After what seemed like forever, the nurse hurried into the room and gave her the pain medication. It made her absolutely loopy before she finally rested and fell into a calm sleep.

By this time, it was 3 o'clock in the morning. The nurse assured us she would sleep now and encouraged us to go home, get a little rest, and come back in the morning. We both left the hospital exhausted and deeply concerned.

I went back the next morning and spent the day with her in the ICU; she slept the entire day. I talked to her, and sometimes she would mumble something and sometimes she would just move her head or hand. While Mom slept, the nurse gathered the necessary information. I gave her mine and my sister's names and told her a little about us.

"She woke up earlier, was alert and talked with me," the nurse reassured.

I was encouraged by what was good news to me and hopeful she would get better. However, while I was there, she slept and slept. Honestly, all I cared about was that she was not in pain. She could wake up and talk to me tomorrow.

I went back to mom's house and later that night I received a call from one of the doctors who informed me that mom would start dialysis the next day. She was readied for the procedure, and it would need to be done 3-4 times a week.

I went back the next morning, there was nothing happening in her room and she seemed to be peacefully asleep. The ICU nurse came in and sat next to me. My heart stopped for a beat when she reached over and took my hand, "Your mother has had a heart attack. We will not be able to start dialysis today. At this point, all we can do is keep her comfortable."

Tears streamed down my face, and a lump as big as my head formed in my throat. "How long?" was all I could manage.

The nurse hugged me and softly replied, "Hours. Probably not through the night."

This was nothing at all like what I expected to hear when I arrived that morning. I went to my mom and choked out, "I love you, Mama." She made a sound, so I knew she heard me, and I took her hand and held it to my face. I didn't want her to go and I had no say in the matter. I felt like the wind had been knocked out of me. I felt so defeated.

I called my sister and aunt and told them the awful news. They both said they would be there as fast as they could. When my sister arrived, I felt overwhelmed and I had to get out for a little bit. My thoughts were all over the place, but all I could focus on was *I need to feed my dog.*

When I drove back to Michigan, after Kristin's graduation, my daughter and her boyfriend drove back with me and we brought my little dog Valentino with us. They stayed a week and were able to visit grandma. When they went home, Val stayed with me.

I told the nurse I was going to leave for a bit but would be back soon. She told me she would call right away if anything changed. Don't ask me why I felt that was the most important thing in the world to me at that moment but maybe I needed to escape, and it was a justification for my escape.

I walked out to the parking lot, settled into dad's Jeep, and turned the keys in the ignition. As I put the Jeep into gear, I noticed the low tire pressure light was glowing. It wasn't on earlier, so I stepped out to check and sure enough, one of the tires was noticeably low.

I got back in and drove to the first gas station and put air in the tire. I had never done this before, and I didn't know how much air to put in, so I just filled it up until it looked good to me. I got back in and started driving and the dang light was still on, so I stopped at the next station and put more air in the tire.

I got back in again and was relieved to see the light finally stayed off, when I heard my phone beeping. I had a voicemail from the hospital. I listened as the nurse told me, "Come back to the hospital as quickly as you can."

It was a 45-minute drive one way between the hospital and the house, but because of that tire, I was less than a mile away. I drove back as quickly as I could, ran through the parking lot, and through the hospital doors towards mom's room. I noticed my nephew was in the lobby and I grabbed him, "We have to hurry to grandma's room."

We rushed through door moments after her last breath. All I could do was hold her and tell her I love her, but she was gone.

I sat there for a little while with my sister, my aunt and nephew. Then I was overcome with the need to just get out of there; I'm sure I was in shock. On my way out, I spoke with the nurse and signed all the necessary paperwork. She explained when the family was ready, she would call the funeral home and I would be notified when they picked her up and I left.

I was wandering around the grocery store carrying dog food when the funeral home director called me to express their condolences and let me know they were on the way to the hospital. I didn't even need dog food. I paid and went home to take care of my little buddy.

That whole night my mind was in disbelief, just three months and three days ago we were all reeling from the loss of my dad.

The next day my sister, my Aunt, and I went to the funeral home, and I was not in the right mind to make one more decision. I told them to do everything for mom that was done for dad. We picked a card, a verse, and my sister and I each picked a song to be played, and we left. Back at the house we selected an outfit for mom and ordered the same floral arrangements we had for dad.

I wanted to honor my Mama in the same way I honored my Daddy, but I couldn't speak at her funeral. I had nothing left in me and quite honestly, I still couldn't believe she was gone, and we were having another funeral. My heart had been broken but now it was shattered.

"He will wipe every tear from their eyes, and death shall be no more, neither shall there be mourning, no crying, nor pain anymore for the former things have passed away."

REVELATION 21:4

THE LESSONS

Chapter Six

The Middle Child

I am the middle child of two middle children. Yes, I have read a few birth order books, but I'll tell you what it means to me. I have an inner married couple who also happen to be my parents that live with my inner child. If you know a couple who have been married for 58 years, you have probably noticed that they sometimes bicker with each other. This is my life, my inner married couple bicker quite often; there are times I try to get away from me/us/them.

I didn't realize how much I am like both of my parents until I spent so much time with them as an adult. I am 50% my mom and 50% my dad. Most people have the characteristics of one parent or the other; I hit the jackpot! My mom gave me my tendency to be co-dependent and I got my coping skills from my dad (in this case drinking). I also received great qualities from them, good work ethic, sense of humor, manners and, most of the time, common sense.

They were married just a few months shy of 58 years; not all of them were easy. I really don't know how they stayed together, except their generation didn't divorce like the generations of today. As often as their marriage was tough and when I say tough, I mean awful, like the use of weapons awful. I remember sitting at the dining table for very long times talking to my dad when he was really drunk just so he and my mom wouldn't argue (fight or worse).

We were not raised in a "Christian home." My church experience was limited to a summer of vacation bible school when I was very young. My sister, who was the oldest, walked us to the church, clutching our dimes to give to the plate lady. I can still remember my first prayer. One night, when I was about 5 or 6, I laid in bed afraid, listening to my parents argue, and prayed, "Dear God, please close all the stores that sell beer. Amen."

In my young little mind, beer was the problem, it was the store's fault my dad could have it, and God could make it go away. That prayer was not answered, and that was the last time I talked to God until I was an adult.

I really don't know how we didn't end up in foster care; except the things they didn't talk about far outweighed the things they did talk about. The fact that my grandfather was a County Sheriff Deputy probably didn't hurt the situation. I am really grateful that I wasn't in the system, but I also think my lack of fear of authority stemmed from not seeing consequences being faced. To this day I have relatives in law enforcement, and I will not involve them in situations I create.

I never had the courage to ask them as an adult about these things that happened when I was very young, but I wish I had. Although there were times of abuse, I really believe that they believed they loved each other, and they were a team.

I have an older sister who married and stayed local; she is still married and has three children. I left home and went to Florida from Michigan when I was 16, not because of them, but because I was 16, knew everything and I was "in love." I married three times and had three children. I had a younger brother who as he became an adult had one issue after another. Sadly, he took his own life and that of another person leaving their child parentless. We did not make things easier for them.

I know every family has struggles at some point, but we always managed to take the hard road whenever possible. My sister and brother's stories are not mine to tell. What I can tell you is leaving home at such a young age really hurt my parents and it is one of my biggest regrets. Oh, there are other regrets but that one is right on top.

My mother's hurt came out as anger and my dad, well he didn't really say anything much to me. At that point he was still drinking, and he didn't quit until later. They both wanted me home and my dad's parents even made a trip down to Florida where I lived and checked on me. I know I hurt a lot of people by leaving.

I told my mom and dad if they made me come home, I would leave again to be with my boyfriend turned husband when I reached the age to get married. One thing I am so grateful for is they never once said, "I told you so," when I was finding out just how hard it was being a "grown-up," and I use that term loosely.

They loved me through everything I went through and put them through. Our relationship was good. In the beginning, I told them what I wanted them to know but as I got older, I'm sure I told them more than they wanted to know.

I later blamed myself for my brother's death; I didn't know what life was like at home after I left but I'm sure my dad expressed his hurt and anger somehow. I'm not sure how that was as I was not told. I know there were mental health issues with my brother; how much my absence contributed to this, I will now never know. I didn't ask, and it wasn't discussed.

I don't believe either of my parents ever got over my brother's death. My mom was always bringing him into conversation, so I know he was always at the forefront of her mind. My dad had quit drinking several years before that, but after my brother's death, I noticed he'd have a beer here and there. Over time it turned into an almost daily occurrence. He would go to the American Legion in town and have a beer or three and maybe a shot of Jim Beam for good measure (coping skills 2.0).

I am still in Florida and as I look back, I believe it was a good move as far as my children were concerned. I feel like I ended, or we are still in the process of ending a generational curse. The cycle of drinking and lives being ruined by substance abuse has been far less destructive and dominant in this next generation than ever before. My kids are fantastic people and have turned into fabulous adults.

As far as being a middle child, I was and still am a buffer. It seems I have the ability to see and empathize with two individual's differences and find myself in the middle trying to make everything better. I just want everyone to be happy and get along. I think that is a wonderful attribute but being that person can be very exhausting. A total people pleaser!

I am working on boundaries and I can read people; I'm very intuitive so I need to listen to my gut and quit putting myself in situations where I am taking on other people's problems. For real, I have enough of my own to keep me plenty busy!

I love being a combination of both of my parents; at times it makes me totally cuckoo but it makes me unique and I believe it has given me the gift to relate to many different people from many walks of life.

"For this reason I bow my knees before the Father, from whom every family in heaven and earth are named."

EPHESIANS 3:14-15

Chapter Seven

The 6th Sense

My dad was a man of few words! Anytime we talked on the phone, he would ask how everyone was doing and ask about the weather. Every now and then, he would tell me a joke he had recently heard or tell me a story about something that happened. He predictably ended our short conversation with, "Well, I'm all out of things to say, I'm going to let you talk to your mom for a while."

My dad enjoyed jokes and laughing. He was literally the bear hug and pull my finger guy. He was rarely serious.

One afternoon we were sitting in the living room watching his beloved Westerns on TV; he leaned over and took my hand. Believe me, he had my attention.

"I really appreciate you being up here helping out," he started. I smiled. I was glad to be there.

He continued and he told me how proud he was of me and how well my kids had turned out. He looked me in the eye and said, "You did a good job, wouldn't you say?"

I couldn't get a word out past the huge lump that had formed in my throat. I nodded in agreement.

"Tracey, remember this. Some people will like you and some people won't and that's OK. What is important is that you have to like yourself. I've lived my life the way I wanted. Some of it was good, some of it was bad. But I've lived life on my own terms and not someone else's."

In 53 years, I think that was the longest conversation my dad and I had ever had at one time. I had waited my whole life to hear that my dad was proud of me. I needed to hear it and my dad needed to say it. I believe my dad was aware that he was reaching the end of his journey on this earth.

The only other lengthy conversation I recall happened shortly after dad got his Jeep in 2009, he had wanted one for years and finally went and picked one out. He was so proud of his Jeep. He called one day and excitedly asked, "You know how motorcycle people wave at each other when they pass?"

"Mmmm-hmmmm," I agreed

"Well, I've decided to start that with my fellow Jeepers. Before I could get a word in, he continued, "Yes, I was out and waved at the first Jeep I passed, but he didn't wave back. The second Jeep I passed, I waved, and he waved back. The third Jeep I passed waved first! Can you believe it, Tracey, that's how quickly it caught on?"

"Only three jeeps! Wow, Dad! That's wildfire impressive!" I shared his enthusiasm.

So yeah, my dad invented the Jeep wave, or at least convinced himself he did. I didn't bother to disagree with him, instead I chose to celebrate with him.

Dad truly did have a "6th sense!!" For him, it was a great sense of humor and he kept it right to the end. We were very grateful for that.

I'm not sure the hospice nurse that came to the house after his last hospital stay felt the same. She arrived with the mandatory questionnaire and worked her way through the required questions.

"Are you eating?" "Some," he replied; he just wasn't feeling hungry, he explained.

"Are you able to get to the bathroom alone?" "Yes," he said.

"Are you able to shower alone?" Dad thought about this one for a moment and Mom and I exchanged a look as he answered, "I haven't tried that yet, but I can stand in front of the sink and wash down as far as possible, and wash up as far as possible, and then I wash possible."

Mom and I knew where this was going, but I thought the poor nurse was going to fall off her chair.

To her credit, she smiled as she collected herself and said, "Okay, well that's good, everything needs to be washed and I can see you have held onto your sense of humor."

I encourage all of you to take my dad's advice, "Don't lose your sense of humor; without it you have nothing."

I can tell you, it helps when you are going through difficult times or maybe a horrible diagnosis, by making memories and leaving behind lighthearted stories to tell and remember your loved ones. I feel so fortunate that my three kids and I have my dad's sense of humor. We are all goofballs, but we sure do enjoy a lot of laughs. God gave us this ability for a reason, and we need to make sure we use it.

"A joyful heart is good medicine,
but a crushed spirit dries up the bones."

PROVERBS 17:22

Chapter Eight

Love thy Neighbor

When my parents built their home in the early '70s the area was very rural. In other words, there was nothing there, and there wasn't anything to do. As you can imagine, as a kid I found it incredibly boring. Oh sure, we played outside, swung on the tire swing, rode our bikes and hoped fervently that someone, someday would move in close by with kids. We learned very quickly not to whine about being bored, the first few times that happened we found ourselves in the garden weeding.

Eventually, we got our wish. The houses were not close to each other so walking or riding bikes was a bit of a hike, but we would enjoy baseball games and hangouts often.

The area developed over the years and more people were building homes out there, but it still had the country feel. The houses were not crowded, the roads were not paved and if you needed something from the store, you could either go a couple of miles to the little store that carried the essentials or drive ten miles "into town."

As an adult when I returned home, I wondered, why did I ever not like living out here? It is so peaceful and beautiful. I would wake up in the early mornings, look out the window and see several deer grazing in the yard. There were always birds at the feeders; in the summer months, mom would make sugar water for the hummingbirds. It was a delight to watch the birds flying in and out to gather their treats.

I also had a new appreciation for the neighbors in the area. I really loved how the neighbors kept to themselves and did their own thing, but still paid attention to each other's routines and kept an eye out for each other. Before my arrival, a huge windstorm had blown through the area. About a week later, one of the neighbors, who walked past my parent's house daily came to the door.

I stepped outside, introduced myself and let her know, "My dad is very ill."

"I had a bad feeling because I know how your dad likes his yard," she replied with concern. "My grandkids are here for a visit and I was wondering if it would be okay to bring them over to pick up the branches for him, but you have to promise not to offer them any money. We want to teach them that helping your neighbors is just what you do, without any expectations of anything in return."

"Well of course," I agreed. "The offer is greatly appreciated, and I promise not to offer the children anything other than our profound thanks."

Sure enough, she showed up later with her tribe. There must have been about five or six children and their mother. They worked their tails off and picked up every twig and branch in the yard. I had asked them to pile it up by the fire pit, and they did. It was a huge pile! They also took two truckloads with them. I was absolutely amazed by this and was refreshed that in today's society there are still families who purposefully encourage such great qualities in the younger generation.

Honestly, the only time my husband and I hear from our neighbors is when there is a complaint about something. There are too many neighborhoods where the neighbors barely even wave and rarely ever make eye contact, so yeah, along with immense gratitude I also felt a sense of sadness.

On the other hand, my dad was nothing but grateful. He couldn't get out there and take care of his yard and it drove him crazy. One morning, I told him I would go out and burn the branches and pick up the pinecones that had fallen. Dad was so very appreciative.

Later, Mom told me the whole time I was out there, Dad kept repeating, "I should be out there helping her."

That's what he did, he took care of things; now he wasn't physically able, and he didn't like it one bit, but expressed gratitude for every offer that came his way.

Over the next couple of weeks, a few more neighbors stopped by to check on my dad. Most would say something like, "I haven't seen your dad out on his tractor. Is he okay?"

The neighbors continued to stop by the whole time I was there, just to check in and see if we were okay, or if we needed anything. That meant so much during such a difficult time.

That neighbor's act of kindness can never be repaid, and I doubt the sweet woman will ever really understand how much she and her family blessed my parents and me that day. I will be forever grateful to her for showing my parents the love they needed right then. It remains a fond memory as well as a reminder to me – to show kindness to others without expectation of anything in return.

"You shall love the Lord your God with all your heart,
with all your soul, and with all your mind.
This is the first and great commandment and the second is like it,
you shall love your neighbor as yourself.

MATTHEW 22:36-39

Chapter Nine

Who Put "FUN" in Dysfunction?

Seriously, family dysfunction is no joke and most families I know have some sort of dysfunction. The definition of dysfunction is, "a deviation from the norms of social behavior in a way regarded as bad." Even Webster didn't make mention of "FUN" in that! I would also say it's an understatement of huge proportions. When going through a difficult family situation (or on a normal Tuesday), there are going to be members of the family who aren't on the same page or are just plain combative.

In my case, while caring for my parents, I had that family member who did not agree with one thing I said or did. Now I tried not to let it bother me, but it really bothered me. There was no help offered, only mean, critical statements and nasty comments during every conversation. There were accusations, judgments, even stories made up about me allegedly doing things that never happened.

You may also find if your family member has grown children, they too may jump on the "hate train" and try to run you over. Just keep in mind it's in the upbringing and we live out what we learn, good or bad. Although much of the talk happened behind my back, when things like this occur in the family you can bet you will hear about them through the family grapevine, and I did.

After a few months of ongoing conflict, I sent a 911 call to my life coach requesting a session, stat! I was not handling it well and I needed to go outside of the family to discuss what was happening. The morning we had our session, I told her that I knew I was a Christ-follower but my "loved one" could turn me into Satan's sidekick in seconds flat. I was not proud of this fact and it wasn't easy to confess I had no self-control, but in order to get the help you need, you have to be brutally honest, UGH! We had a very good conversation about responding vs reacting.

A reaction and a response may look exactly alike, however, they feel different. A reaction is instant. It's driven by beliefs, biases, and is on some level a defense mechanism. A response will come more slowly. It's based on information from both the conscious and unconscious mind. A response takes into consideration the well-being of not only you but those around you. It weighs the long-term effects and stays in line with your core values.

Even though I understood what she was telling me it was still super challenging to put in action. I truly tried to make amends and smooth things out, but the more I tried, the worse the criticism and anger became.

So how do you deal with that when you're already under a tremendous amount of stress? Distance……………………lots and lots of distance whenever possible, minimal conversation and determining when it's absolutely necessary to contact the person or if it's a situation that can be handled on your own. Depending on the situation you are in, the position you have been given, and how you choose to respond, this could be easy, or this could be hard.

I hadn't expected both my parents to pass so closely together, and once they had, I knew my next task at hand was to take care of their estate. When I hired a realtor and started boxing things up for the estate sale, the anger toward me was amplified. I was told it was too soon and as far as they were concerned, it could all sit there for 10 years.

I knew I couldn't be there to maintain the property; I also knew no one else would either. I had seen proof of that on several occasions; I could not count on the family. I had been away from my husband and children for months and I missed them terribly. So, I went to it and did what I had to do.

Putting a price on the possessions my parents obviously treasured was extremely difficult, especially knowing that whatever price I put on each item, an interested buyer would ask me to lower the price by 75%. These "things" were all I had left of my parents, and in my mind, they were priceless. Once again, my dear, wise coach gave me a different perspective and told me, "Those things don't have a heartbeat or a soul. They are things that did their job while your parents used and enjoyed them and now, your mom and dad would be glad to know someone else has the opportunity to use and enjoy these things."

That put my mind at a certain level of ease to get through it; it did not change the magnitude of the job. My parents had named me to take care of the estate, and even though the nonsense continued, I found an ally and the strength to do what needed to be done.

You may find you are extremely blessed and have family members who will sacrifice their time and energy to help. My aunt was amazing and helped me with so much, especially the estate sale, which was no small task. It took all of our time around our work schedules for weeks. I am most grateful for her emotional support. She had a ton of things going on in her family and yet she made sure she was there for me; you cannot repay that kind of generosity. We were close before all of this, but after our time together the bond became even stronger.

Unfortunately, the distance between some of my family has

grown to the point of absolutely no contact because the relationships were making me physically ill. This was a very hard decision, because I was taught as I was growing up that family was always there for family. I came to the realization that if family was hurtful and uncaring, distance is sometimes the only way to protect yourself, and that's OK.

I haven't stopped loving my dysfunctional family; I have forgiven them, and I will continue to pray for them as always. Knowing you are at the end of a relationship with the very people you believed you would always stand side-by-side with and have each other's backs is very difficult to accept. It is sad to realize that any semblance of a loving family unit has been destroyed.

During all of this, I recalled the many conversations my parents and I had as to how they wanted things handled. The easiest way for me to get through this was to keep focused on what I knew mom and dad wanted. Today, I have peace in my heart knowing I honored their wishes.

"Let all bitterness and wrath and anger and clamor and slander be put away from you, along with all malice. Be kind to one another, tenderhearted, forgiving one another, as God in Christ forgave you."

EPHESIANS 4:31-32

Chapter Ten

Army of Advocates

We are not in control of our lives no matter how hard we try to be or think we are. The path of life is full of obstacles to be overcome, life situations which must be faced, and unplanned circumstances (daily, if your life is anything like mine). People show their true colors in the midst of major life events – when times are difficult, when an emergency arises, even during times of success -when praise or applause is called for.

An advocate is a person who upholds, supports and even promotes and champions for you at the worst and best of times. The people you surround yourself with need to have your best interest at hand, just as you have their best interest first and foremost. It is so important to know who is in your Army. Before I understood this, I did not practice safe and healthy boundaries.

Boy were my eyes opened wide when my family faced this most heartbreaking life event – turns out there were several kinds of people in my Army.

There were the ones who weren't able to help because their own lives were so full of commitments, and there were some not willing to sacrifice any of their time or interrupt their routine in any way.

There were the ones who dropped everything and came to help, without even knowing what it might be they were helping with.

So many of my friends were in a different state, yet they faithfully called, sent a text or note through social media to let me know they were thinking of us, praying for us or just letting us know they loved us. That meant so much to me and my family.

I also found some of my people were there for my support of them, but unable or unwilling to be supportive of me.

My biggest supporters were my immediate family. My husband, Larry, had already experienced the loss of his parents. Even before Dad was hospitalized, he encouraged me to go up and help, "Your parents need you now, like you needed them fifty years ago."

Whoa, that was so real to me.

I left for Michigan; Larry stayed home to work and take care of my menagerie of 3 dogs, 2 cats and 2 pigs. My dad often teased me that I was a descendant of the Clampetts (of the Beverly Hillbillies, specifically Ellie Mae). Maybe I should have mentioned the kids first, but Larry also made himself available when they needed him.

Larry called a couple times a day for updates, I would say, "Hello," he would say, "Hellooo," and wait to hear what was going on with mom, dad or me and whatever the news of the day happened to be. His calls were such a big thing to me, keeping everyone updated is a job in itself. He never asked when I was coming home, he only let me know that he missed me and continually encouraged me to take my time and do whatever I needed to do.

Larry gave me a gift that I will never be able to reciprocate – the most precious gift of time with my parents. That is just how selflessly he loves me, and I am incredibly blessed to be his wife.

The two of us literally put our lives on hold for all those days, only concentrating on my parents and what needed to be done.

I can tell you there is something special about getting right out of the way and thinking of only those with you. It is an amazing feeling and fills your heart fuller than anything you can do with yourself in mind.

My kids, Gary, Corey and Kristin, showed me they were capable young adults who could put others before themselves. If you know more than 10 people, you know there are people who try to make everything about them and do not have the capability to get themselves out of the way for anyone. Knowing how very important it was for me to take care of their Grandma and Grandpa, my kids took a step back and put themselves on the back burner. This gesture caused my heart to swell and the love I had for my children grew. I had not even thought this was possible, but I was prouder than ever of each one of them!

Kristin graduated from high school that year; I missed so many exciting events of that momentous year, including prom. Thanks to technology we Face-Timed while she was getting ready. She totally rocked a long, sleeveless red gown with silver sequins and sparkling crystals adorning the high-necked bodice, just beautiful. Her blonde hair was pulled back in front and curls cascaded down her back. She was absolutely stunning! Her boyfriend, very handsome in a black tuxedo with a coordinating red vest and bowtie, presented her with a lovely wrist corsage. They looked like a celebrity couple!

My eyes misted with happy tears as the call ended. My dad turned to me with concern on his face and asked, "You're missing her prom?" I shook my head in acknowledgment and he looked so sad.

I knew he felt bad and that was the last thing I wanted. Not wanting to make it a big deal, I assured him, "Dad, you know how it is with teens. She'll be spending the weekend with her friends. I probably saw more of her today than I would have if I were home."

I truly had a sense of peace. Two of my girlfriends were with Kristin, pampering her in preparation for the big night. The hair, the makeup, the dress – they captured precious moments and there were tons of photos to revisit when I went home. Again, a very wonderful gift, selflessly given.

I knew I was right where I was supposed to be. My needs and desires were provided for and God carried me through every single day I was there. I made it through each day by His strength, not mine. I understood so many things I never gave thought to before- medical, financial, retirements, and insurance. I was able to manage my parents' appointments, speak to doctors, and actually do what needed to be done once I got them home. Somehow, I just got (or God) it! Normally, I would be out of my mind with anxiety, but I felt a calm knowing. His presence was palpable.

I had to shop and cook!! This is not something I was used to. Larry did all the shopping, meal planning and cooking. I may or may not have had a meltdown right in the middle of the produce section at the Meijer store. It is pretty stressful to shop for someone else and spend their money on groceries.

There were times I was surprised at what I was able to do physically to help mom and dad. Daily, I assisted them in the bathroom, in and out of the vehicle or getting them to their doctor appointments. When they were very weak, the responsibilities increased, and I helped them dress. I became their strength only because God gave me His.

While I was my parents' caregiver and after the loss of dad and mom, there was so much to do that I knew nothing about or had no experience in. I hired contractors to build a ramp for my mom for when she came home so she would be able to get in the house with her wheelchair or walker, to check the foundation in their second garage, took care of someone else's finances, auto sales, title transfers, and an estate sale that I could have never pulled off without my Aunt. The sale of my dad's gun collection nearly put me over the edge; I've always hated guns.

My Aunt knew a couple of guys who were very knowledgeable in this area. They came by the house with their books about guns and their value. Except for the handling of said guns, I appreciated their expertise greatly. Did I mention I hated guns?

I knew nothing about the logistics of selling guns and called the Sheriff department to ask questions. A few days passed and God placed two of the most amazing Deputies in my path. Woohooo, thank you, Jesus! They were gun enthusiasts and knew everything I didn't. They took the time to help me find the value of and price each gun.

Before they arrived, I was completely lost! This wasn't life or death, but they were heroes to me! They gave generously of their time and knowledge and refused to accept anything in return other than my appreciation-no payment, no trade, not even an item from the Estate Sale. It was truly a privilege and an awesome learning experience.

During that time, I acquired more than just knowledge; I learned to respect the guns and became intrigued by them. I have since taken all the necessary classes and currently own my first gun Allow me to brag for a second – I even outshot my husband during the "firing of a gun" section of the classes. Another wonderful gift, which I cannot repay!

God also gave me authentic confidence that I didn't possess before. I had so much alone time, I learned a ton about myself -

things I knew were assets and valuable traits, things I knew needed some work and things that just had to go. I wish I could say God fixed it all, but that's not how He rolls. Oh sure, He can fix anything and do anything, Afterall, He is a miracle maker.

He has a way of making us very aware of things that may not be "His way" and need to be changed. He then steps back and waits to see what we do with that awareness. He wants us to grow and mature. We need to do that work on our own. There are many things He will not do for us because His love for us is so great he wants us to become the people He knows we can be and carry out the plans He has for us.

The awareness doesn't come to you automatically, you become aware after you've been through it. You are able to look back and go, "Oh yeah," and you gain a sense of clarity.

God has given me so many insights over the last five years. I have learned God will surround you with the right Army if you surrender to Him and He will lead your Army on a path that will get you to the other side of obstacles, life situations and unplanned circumstances. You just have to trust and have faith.

Think about it, when we grow to be what God made us to be, we will be in the most phenomenal place and have eternity to enjoy it!

"For I know the plans I have for you," declares the Lord, "Plans to prosper you and not to harm you, plans to give you hope and a future."

JEREMIAH 29:11

Epilogue

Home Bittersweet Home

I didn't know it at the time, but my whole life was about to change on December 31, 2013. It started with a bonfire, the flames of which have burned in my heart since that fateful night. How the bonfire brought about that change is still a mystery to me but let me tell you what I do know.

God prepared me to answer the call when the phone rang on February 8, 2017, the first day of an unexpected journey. When I left for Michigan the next day, I had no idea I was starting out on a journey that would end with the loss of my parents. But God gave me His strength and stayed with me every step of the way. He continues to give me His strength to live without people I never considered I would have to learn to live without.

My parents taught me important life lessons right up to their final days. I have witnessed people being selfless, but now I know what it's like to be selfless, what it feels like, what it looks like and how rewarding it can be. My mom and dad taught me how to get myself right out of the way and to give all I have to someone else. When you are selfless in the name of love, let me tell you, you will want to make this part of your everyday life.

Knowing that you are at the end of a chapter in your life, needless to say, is a very hard adjustment. The process continues and life must go on. There are many necessary tasks to complete and many "things" that have to be resolved.

We gathered my parents' belongings for an estate sale. It took three grueling weeks to prepare for, and we held it for two weekends. After the sale, there were still many decisions to make. Some things were given away, some things were donated. Some things were kept by my sister and me.

The house was put up for sale and that too was very difficult. I watched people come in and walk around the house that my mom and dad had made a home and kept up for over forty years. I listened to the comments to their realtors about what they could change. I wanted nothing changed. I wanted my parents back. This was an awful nightmare I wanted to wake up from. I could not get my head and heart to grasp the reality I was living. It wasn't normal, nothing was normal. I was alone doing things I didn't want to be doing but was committed to following through with the wishes my parents had put into place.

I was in a state of limbo, but after the estate sale, I just knew there was no reason to stay and wait for the house to sell. I was torn, I needed my safe place, but I was afraid to leave. The finality of it was overwhelming, and I was concerned about leaving the house unattended. I called the Sheriff's office and explained the situation, and they promised to check on the house until it sold.

My decision was made. It was time to leave and return home to my family in Florida. I called Larry, "I'm ready to come home."

"I'm on my way," was his quick reply. True to his word, he left immediately.

A weight on the bed woke me in the middle of the night. Larry's familiar arms surrounded me, and I felt safe again.

The next day, I arranged with our realtor to complete the sale of the house through the mail. With all of the details taken care of, we were ready to go. My aunt and cousins came to see us off.

On the 198th day, with Larry driving a 26-foot moving truck

filled to the hilt, my dad's Jeep in tow, and me following in my mom's car, we started for home. I remember driving down the driveway, looking at my childhood home in the rearview mirror, the home I went to every time I took a vacation, the home I thought I would call home until the day I died, and realizing I would no longer have this place to call home. Right then, whatever part of my heart was still intact cracked.

My prayer for all of you is, if you are going through a difficult life event, an experience you think might be more than you can handle and you haven't looked to God for answers or guidance, please give it a try. He wants to wrap you up in love.

God gave me strength and courage, He carried me when I didn't have an ounce of energy and finally the peace of knowing I did all I could with the knowledge I had. If asked, prior to this, if I would be able to be a caregiver to my parents and get them from this life to the next, I would have to be honest and say, "Absolutely not!" When we think we are not strong enough, capable enough, or just plain enough, that's when God gets our attention, somehow. If we surrender to Him, He will be faithful to us and guide our way. Will He make it easy? No, but knowing we have a relationship with Christ is a very strong bond and if God is with us, who can be against us?

"With promises like this to pull us on, dear friends, let's make
a clean break with everything that defiles us or distracts us,
both within and without. Let's make our entire lives fit and
holy temples for the Worship of God."

2 CORINTHIANS 7:1

In Memory of

My 11-Pound Superhero

I wanted a little Shih Tzu in the worst way. On Valentine's Day, 2003, I visited a breeder's home and met my special little man. His siblings barked and jumped in excitement. I enjoyed the puppy antics, but I noticed a sweet little guy sitting quietly on his own and immediately knew he was mine.

Valentino, aka Rudog Valentino, became a part of our family that day. The kids and I adored him. He answered to Valentino, Val, Valie, Li'l Man, and Sweet Boy. He was never more than a few inches away from me at any given time.

He was with me through the worst relationship I ever experienced which led to the breaking up of my family, much drinking, domestic violence, emotional abuse, and even a couple of arrests. Believe me, when I made bad decisions, I went all out!

During my drinking days, Valentino sat with me on the back porch, never letting me out of his sight. I set up two chairs, one for him and one for me. He patiently sat by my side waiting to lick the condensation off the empty bottles. I often joked, "He drinks the outside, and I drink the inside."

Fast forward to the writing of this book, as I had told you, after I came down for Kristin's graduation, Valentino went on his first long road trip, all the way to Michigan. Of course, he was the perfect little traveler. He mostly laid on his back, snoring loudly, except to take potty breaks and eat. After the kids left to get back to Florida and prepare for college, it was Val and I, while mom was in the nursing home. He was even allowed to go visit grandma with me. When grandma came home, she snuck him snacks, allowed him on the furniture and he even got to sleep in the bed. This went to his head and whenever he was doing something he wasn't allowed to do at home, he gave me very smug looks when we made eye contact.

When we came home to Florida, I noticed he was having dribbling problems. After visiting the vet, I purchased doggie diapers. We called them man pants so he could keep his dignity intact. Several vet appointments later, we discovered his kidneys were failing and his health was declining.

At this point, he had been by my side for 16 years. I bought special food for a renal diet, which he would not eat. He refused anything other than chicken and rice, but he was still eating, drinking and going to the bathroom. I believed things were looking up.

He seemed stable and with him next to me I continued to write the book. I had two chapters to write, Daddy and Mama. I kept pushing it off or there was something holding me back, I was stuck.

Val also lost his hearing and his vision worsened. We worked out hand signals for commands. He knew when I wanted him to follow me. He could not be the line leader because he bumped into things. Outside he used the fence as a guide.

Sadly, Valentino was showing signs of increased failing, more vet visits were made, and they confirmed the worst. It would only be a matter of time.

One day I noticed he couldn't get his back end up into his bed and dragged it a little when he walked. I called the vet and told them, "I think it's time."

They told me to bring him in. He and I held hands/paws and he laid his head on my hand all the way there. I was distracted driving for sure, holding his paw and bawling all the way.

During the procedure, I couldn't let him go. His eyes pleaded with me. The vet came in and asked if I was ready. "No," I said, "but he is."

She gave him a small injection and he became very relaxed and sleepy. He laid his head on my hand. She told me, "I'm going to give him the rest of the anesthesia," and listened to him with her stethoscope. After a few seconds, she looked at me and said, "He's gone."

Even after all I'd been through, I didn't think it was possible for a person to cry so much.

We arranged for him to be cremated and a plaster to be made of his paw print. All I could do was cry and miss him, while I waited to pick up his paw print and all that was left of him in a precious little box.

My li'l man was gone, and I was left with all these feelings of loss I could not get control over swirling in my gut. The feelings didn't lessen with time, they intensified.

You see, while I was in Michigan taking care of everything, I did not allow myself to grieve. Of course I was sad, of course I missed my parents and shed tears at their passing, but I had things to take care of. I was very busy getting things done so I could come home to my family.

Once I was home, I was back in my "normal" environment, and I would have very rough days but would push those feelings down, still not allowing myself to grieve.

I believe Valentino knew he had to leave me so I could heal. Even in his death, he was taking care of me. I have started the grieving process, and somehow found the courage to write the hardest chapters, crying and allowing the hurt to surface through the process.

And so, I offer to you, my journey, the lessons learned, and the courage to heal in memory of my 11-pound Superhero.

Valentino, I miss you as if a part of my own self is missing. You were the best little companion a person could ask for. I couldn't have chosen a better puppy. I take comfort in knowing you are being spoiled rotten by grandma and grandpa.

You are forever in my heart.

Valentino Batchelder

February 2003-May 2019

If I speak the languages of men and of angels, but do not have love, I am a sounding gong or a clanging cymbal.

If I have the gift of prophesy, and understand all mysteries and all knowledge, and if I have all faith, so that I can move mountains, but do not have love, I am nothing.

And if I donate all my goods to feed the poor, and if I give my body to be burned, but do not have love, I gain nothing.

Love is patient; love is kind. Love does not envy; is not boastful; is not conceited; does not act improperly; is not selfish; is not provoked; does not keep a record of wrongs; finds no joy in unrighteousness, but rejoices in truth; bears all things, believes all things, hopes all things, endures all things.

Love never ends. But as for prophesies, they will come to an end; as for languages, they will cease; as for knowledge, it will come to an end.

For we know in part, and we prophesy in part.
But when the perfect comes, the partial will come to an end.

When I was a child, I spoke like a child, I thought like a child, I reasoned like a child.

When I became a man, I put aside childish things.
For now we see indistinctly, as in a mirror,
but then face to face. Now I know in part,
but then I will know fully, as I am fully known.

Now these three remain:
faith, hope, and love.
But the greatest of these is love.

1 CORINTHIANS 13:1-13

99

Letter from the Author

Dear Reader,

The Journey I have shared with you has changed my life completely. It has made me realize my value, to cherish the precious gift of life and not to waste a second on things that won't help me or someone else grow. I no longer work for simply a paycheck; I work to help others see their value and I am a hope giver.

I have experienced many things in my life and needed someone to be there for me. At times, it seemed that no one was available. I will be that person for others. I will be that cheerleader for people who find themselves in situations they've gotten themselves into or ended up in due to their family structure or other circumstances beyond their control. I can truly relate to some devastating consequences based on my own choices or the choices that have been made for me.

It is important to me to help others learn The Lessons I have learned so far, to show others how to create boundaries and to use your voice when things are happening to you that are not okay.

All of us can find ourselves in dark places, but we don't have to stay there. I have a light I can shine brightly when others are lost on what looks like a dark and hopeless path. I will walk with you every step of the way to find hope.

I am currently working on my second book and have recently completed the coursework to become a Peer Recovery

Specialist.

I'd love to hear from my readers. I can be contacted by email at traceybatchelder198days@gmail.com.

Your Hope Giver,

Tracey Batchelder

Author, Certified Life Coach, and Peer Recovery Specialist

Follow 198 Days @traceybooks

https://www.facebook.com/traceybooks/

www.ingramcontent.com/pod-product-compliance
Lightning Source LLC
LaVergne TN
LVHW091227080426
835509LV00009B/1198